Smokey of the Migraines

Michael McInnis

Nixes Mate Books
Allston, Massachusetts

Copyright © 2017 Michael McInnis

Book design by d'Entremont
Cover photograph from the collection of Lauren Leja

All rights reserved. This book or any portion thereof may not be reproduced or used in any manner whatsoever without the express written permission of the publisher except for the use of brief quotations in a book review or scholarly journal.

Sections of this poem appeared in *Your One Phone Call*.

Thanks to Lauren Leja whose squinting keeps me from falling back on my own worst instincts. Thanks to Annie and Philip for sharing this vision. Thanks to Heather Sullivan and Jay Miner. Finally, thanks to Andrew Guthrie for 35 years of friendship discussing art and literature and music.

ISBN 978-0-9993971-2-1

Nixes Mate Books
POBox 1179
Allston, MA 02134
nixesmate.pub/books

I am a dance myself
a high step
a leap
before history & hands
the american wish
sleek & slicked w/guns & money

Dillnger: the Name is Dillinger – Todd Moore

Smokey of the Migraines

Smokey and Lefty
are down
the union hall
talking to Sully.
They want no shows.
They want Sully
to pay up,
Sully to
arrange for
Lefty's brother-in-law
to work.
Sully can't do it.
Smokey says to him
he says you can't
or won't you bastard.
Smokey sees Sully
ain't going
to oblige
them ain't
playing along.
No matter the reason
Smokey don't like

people who can't
or won't.
Smokey don't find
their recalcitrance funny.
Lefty looks longways –
his mouth is
always drooping –
when Smokey says
recalcitrance.

Where'd ya learn that,
Lefty says.

Father Xavier.
He says to me
he says ya know
Smokey your boys,
the boys you sent
me last week they
wouldn't kneel and
pray with me,
pray on the hard
floor of the
rectory mudroom.
ten *Hail Marys*,

an *Act of Contrition*
nothing difficult
nothing no
Catholic boy
growing up in the
projects couldn't
recite after confession.
Recalcitrant
they was Smokey
he says to me.

Lefty don't care
what a pedophile
junkie says,
the pervert fucker.
He wants a job for
the bastard his
sister married
that no good
half polack
half Irish
dipshit.
At least he ain't no
dagowop bastard
Lefty had whispered

to his mother
at the wedding.
But now this jerk,
this recalcitrant
Sully ain't
letting go
of what he has,
of what he owes
and Smokey's
not haven't it.

Lefty senses it.

Lefty tastes it.

Lefty feels it.

Heat and steam curdling
off the nicotine
stained drop ceiling.

Lefty knows it.

If Smokey
don't act soon,

don't kill this fucker
leave his body in the
mud of the bay
then Smokey's migraine's
gonna go supernova.

Lefty smells it.

Sulfur,
sparks,
ozone
coming
off Smokey.

The migraine's
burning inside
Smokey's head.

All the
dead light
in the room,
the murdered
light,
shatters
at the edge

of Smokey's
visible spectrum.

Sully's whiny voice
pile drives deeper
into Smokey's head.
Outside,
a commuter train
whistle blows
and rattles
the windows.

The migraine takes
Smokey outside
his body
where he exists
far from
the reach
of life,
of love,
beyond the polished
black metal of the
Glock 9 he shoves
in Sully's mouth,
chipping a tooth

and cutting
the fucker's lips.
Smokey smells
the piss soaking
Sully's pants.

The migraine
gets Smokey thinking
of every mother
fucker who
thought he knew
better, who wouldn't
give up what he owed.

Why does
every fuckhead
think
he can do what
he wants,
hold on
to what
he owes,
what he's obligated
to give up
whether its jobs

or money,
drugs
or pussy.

The migraines
speak to Smokey
in tongues
he barely understands.
They tell him
stories that
have no meaning.

The migraines
talk at him in
incomprehensible
words that
remind him
of the adult
voices on *Peanuts*
specials.

The migraine
is a ghost
whispering
of death

and night
and blood.

The migraine
is Jackson Pollack
severing occipital
nerves
with paint.

The migraine
is the
plutonium
taste of meth
down the back
of the throat.

The migraine
is a creature
living in Smokey's neck
reaching up
through his
brain
and pulling
each eye back
back down.

The migraine
is an itch
beneath the
straps of a
back pack
straining with
the weight
of its terrible truth,
of nails and screws,
bits of rock,
pieces of glass
and broken marbles.

The migraine
is smoke and
burnt flesh,
burnt wood,
burnt plastic,
as if a scream
had a smell,
a taste,
a touch.

The migraine
is the splatter

of paint,
an ocular
darkness
of color
and sound.
Pollack,
again,
in the garage
in East Hampton,
shattering
his brains
out on
canvas.

The migraine
is the
mortification
of flesh
glazed with auras
and sounds
heard rumbling
under the skin,
rifling through
marrow.

The migraine
is a killing field,
manured with
the blood of
shell-shocked men.

The migraine exists
outside
ecclesiastical
boundaries,
a leftover
of Purgatory,
lingering
to plague
the unholy,
the lost ones
who left the Church
or turned away
from the light.

Smokey
can't seek
the light
because
the migraine

is light,
diffused,
catholic,
exquisite
as if the blue
of Smokey's irises
is a laceration.

Smokey hesitates,
a coronal hammer,
a brief pause,
a shadow on his grave,
like glaciers
stopped at
the edge
of the continent,
like the planet
shifting,
like the tides
frozen between
migraines
and screaming.

In that pause,
that hesitation

Smokey knows
there exists all
the time he needs
for him
to get back
in the car
and drive back
through the tolls,
back to an ocular hell
of pain
and auras
and screaming
that is the migraine,
to drive
back to the edge
of the bridge,
back to a slow
suicide, an
invisible,
inevitable
slide
to death
as if the
jump off
the bridge

was horizontal
and took years
to complete,
where only the
screaming remained,
burning,
as if the migraine
had caught fire
and the ferric
smell
of blood,
was a weight
too heavy
to hang over
a city
where
no planes
scream like
rockets,
where no
alarms sound,
where no
firefighters
climb a
thousand stairs,

where no
bodies fall
and hit
the concrete
ground like so
many bundles of
2x4's,
where no buildings
collapse
or rip apart,
where fragments
of glass do not
ink the sky
with a freighted
penmanship,
where no vans
cartwheel through
pedestrians,
set adrift in a
solar system
searching for life,
where no women
crawl on the
sidewalk,
trying to stand,

to find purchase
on a brick wall,
falling back,
always falling back,
never understanding
that her hand
is missing,
where no
pink bicycles,
her rider spirited away,
are left
at the side
of the road,
a traffic light
flashing red,
green and yellow,
where no
vehicles stopped at
odd angles to each
other and the
geometry of the street,
where no drivers push
open shattered doors,
face speckled with a
pox draining down

his shirt
where no
colors, leeched
out of the night,
become
ligaments of memory,
of sacrifice,
of lost time,
where no
weddings
or buses
or marathons,
varnished with
a wicked wind,
disappear into
the maw of gravity,
where there are
no paintings
to finish,
no poems
to write,
no sound
tracks
to compose,
where Smokey

is no longer
haunted by
the polluted soil
and withered
by the cold winds
of a city
on a hill;
in that pause,
that hesitation
before the
trigger is pulled
before the
button is pushed,
before the
boxcutter is swung,
before the
dustbin of history
is emptied,
before the punks
and anarchists
and situationists
spell the word

s p e c t a c l e

a filtered signal
darkens the edges
of Smokey's senses,
each shutting down
except the screaming,
the migraine
still alive,
the stars still
pinwheeling above
in the murkiness
of a blackhole
where Smokey,
at last,
understands
the nature of time.

But Smokey can't
squeeze his head
the way he likes
when he's home in bed,
pressing his palms
into each temple
like the book press
that Uncle Fester
used to cure

his headaches
on *The Addam's Family*.
All the kids
laughed at that.
But Smokey
knew it worked,
knew it helped
shut out the explosions
that threatened
to overwhelm him,
threatened to send
him down a pit
where only pain
and nausea
and fire
and eternal
damnation waited.

Smokey don't notice
he's lost in the migraine,
time traveling,
to Dealey Plaza
where the sun never sets
for the king
returned,

for the king
sacrificed,
for the king
kissing
his boots,
the Book Depository
a new capitol,
and the hundred years
between two
kings and the letters
of their names,
the mountain ranges,
latitudes and
assassins.
Sic semper tyrannis!

Smokey
time-traveling
through the
migraine,
through ropes
of light, to
Marat's bath,
water on the tile,
footsteps

in the hall,
a ghost,
a shadow,
an angel,
an assassin,
always assassins,
the knife
drinking blood.
J'ai tué un homme!
I killed
one man
to save
thousands!

Smokey
time traveling
to the shabby
Mexico City room
Trotsky called home,
to Constantinople
when the sun bled,
to the end of a
dusty alley in
Ojinaga
where the old Gringo,

the old *viejo loco* had
come to meddle,
to exorcise
the ghosts of
Shiloh,
where dust haloed
his eyes and
words kept spilling
out of the holes
in his chest,
where his
blood was tattooed
with dust,
the bitter
dust of Villa's
revolution,
a glorious
lost cause
chased across
the desert.
Villa,
who would
never ride to
rescue Smokey,
who would

never escape
the barking dogs,
and gunshots,
and dead horses,
the frugality
of a canister
shot cutting
down whole
platoons,
the dust of war.

At the birth of
Mary Shelley's
monster
Smokey stood
and shook
with recognition
knowing only
ice and madness.

Smokey urged
the Beothuk
to push
Leif Erickson
back into the sea.

He watched men
attain the
knowledge of gods
and burn holes
in the sky over
White Sands,
Hiroshima,
Nagasaki
and Bikini.

Smokey armed Metacom
and counseled him
to raze New England,
knowing
the Pokanoket
would eventually
lose.

Tituba created
poultices for
Smokey's
migraines,
for the fear,
for the devils
of Salem.

In the attic
on Kennedy's farm –
again the king –
Smokey watched
John Brown hand
out pikes to his men,
telling them
they were about
to do the Lord's work.

Smokey's with
Traven
during the cruel, joyous
summer of 1914,
before the
desiccated landscapes
of France,
before the archaeology
of mud and
blood and
the gristle of men
snuffed out
in the *frontgraben*,
before the dead
right eye of migraines,

the dashed skulls,
the rats and
the little corporal,
the ocular
migraine
hanging
on the wire,
trussed up as if
crucifixion
and the green
glazing of gas
were a defense
against mutiny
and yet more
migraines.

Smokey's with
Traven
digging
skull fragments
out of the ruins
of Verdun,
a boot with
toe bones
from the banks

of the Marne,
a punctured helmet
in the woods
near Charlevaux.

Smokey's back
with the witch
at Topsfield Fair
who told him
he had the
longest life line
she had ever seen.
That was when
Smokey started
to believe he
couldn't be touched,
that bullets
would pass
through him
and the Feds
would look
the other way
while he
and Lefty
raked it in.

Smokey says to Sully,
he says
I can't be touched.
I am un fucking
touchable
you hear me
you fucking fuck
motherfucker.

The migraine
needs more than
a long life line,
it needs pressure,
it needs quiet
and darkness.

Smokey
once asked
Father Xavier
whether the migraines
were penance,
punishment from
God
for Smokey's sins,
for turning

a blind eye to
the priest's preying
on the lost boys
from the projects,
for the shots of smack
he gave the priest
whenever
Father Xavier
came back from
Suffolk Downs
broke and dejected,
straying from
the protection
of Mary the
Mother of God.

Smokey wonders
if he might find
salvation
in the migraines
after all.

Free the pain,
do penance for
all the killings,

for letting the
Feds take
Johnny Longneck
and for sticking
his gun in
Mairead's cunt
after she
slapped his face.

A migraine
won't change
the sound
mud makes
when it sucks
a body
in with
a watery gasp.
Smokey always
liked that sound,
amazed
the mud acted
like a vacuum
as if the mud
had become
a gate to a

ghost city,
a city of cow paths
and witches,
and the torments
of hell,
a city of
oceans and
pirates,
mutineers,
red Indians,
praying Indians,
a city
founded on a
catechism of
catastrophe.
In that city,
in the clam flats,
on the shores of
drumlins
and rivers that
turn in on
themselves,
the Feds'd
need back-hoes
to dig up,

from the oily muck,
the bones of
Smokey's migraines.

When we kill
this fuck,
Smokey says to Lefty,
he can't go in
where everyone else is.
Don't want people
to think we're lazy
or dumb
or something.
We can run him
out to sea.
Go fish for cod
off Nova Scotia.

Why not smuggle
him into Nova Scotia.

Guns,
drugs
and bodies,
a smuggler

can handle anything
just like a salesmen
should be able
to sell anything,
like a man
of the cloth
can absolve
the sins of murderers,
thieves
and housewives
all on the same day.
Each sinner
says an
Act of Contrition.
Each ready
and willing
to commit more sins.

No absolution,
no dispensation,
no sin eaters
can cure a migraine.

Smokey feels nauseous,
his skin paper white,

but his hand steady.
All his other senses
shuddering
and shaking.
The florescent
lights bleeding
through the migraine,
skinning and
scraping
the inside of
Smokey's
skull,
wire-brushing
his eyes.

Sully
whimpering,
sees no flashes
of his life,
offers no regrets,
knows no need to
apologize.
The Glock,
now full of blood
and spit

tastes like
a rosary,
like salvation,
like the red
wine of Christ's
blood
as if the gun
is pure and
transmogrified.

The ocean,
just over
the Expressway,
is a luxury,
a monastery
of islands
in the bay,
drumlins
rising up from the
clam beds and
mud flats and
beaches of
torpedoed
glass,
shells,

rusted rafts and
submarine nets.

How many miles
to Nova Scotia,
Smokey says.

Lefty shrugs
his shoulders,
far enough,
he says.

Far enough
for this fuck
to feed
the sharks,
far enough
to the edge
of the continent,
to the edge
of the world,
far enough
for this fuck
to feed all
the sea monsters

and
white whales,
far enough
for drowned sailors
trapped in
Davy Jones'
Locker
far enough
for Shellbacks,
far enough
for shipwrecks
and cannibals,
far enough
for the migraine.

The migraine
is a 9mm
under Smokey's
pillow.

The migraine
is the guts
of a burner
phone on the floor.

The migraine
is a whiskey bottle
on the nightstand.

The migraine
is a dream,
a nightmare
become
blackness,
as if Smokey,
falling out
buildings
on fire,
on a planet with
violent weather
full of
electrical charges,
and oceans painting
the land black,
had discovered
burning stars,
solar flares
and migrainous
caverns.

The migraine
is a fall
from grace.

The migraine
is Smokey's
sister left
for dead,
a needle in her arm,
behind the old
fire station,
young boys
poking sticks
at her,
trying to wake her,
testing
their knowledge
of science and God
in a city under
a bridge,
an Indian village
with clear, cold
spring water
turned foul,
polluted
with oil farms
and turpentine,

and varnishes,
and tankers,
and drawbridges,
and war,
and burning frigates.

The migraine
is a rag shop fire,
a conflagration
charring a city,
turning black
the sides of buildings,
back porches,
parlors, and
during supper,
the faces of children
and mothers
and grandmothers.

The migraine
is a vision.

The migraine
is vision.

The migraine
exists without color.

The migraine
is a vocabulary
without words,
without sounds.

The migraine
is a revolution,
a manifesto of
pain.

The migraine
is a running sea,
a *Fata Morgana,*
an ocular
horizon.

The bullet
shatters the back
of Sully's
coruscating
head.

The migraine
is Smokey.

About the Author

Michael McInnis lives in Boston and served six years in the Navy chasing white whales and Soviet submarines. He was the founder of the Primal Plunge, Boston's first and only bookstore dedicated to zine and underground culture and small press literature. When he is not writing, Michael spends his time making furniture and composing ambient soundtrack music. His poetry and short fiction has appeared or is forthcoming in *Chiron Review*, *The Commonline Journal*, *Cream City Review*, *Naugatuck Review*, *One-Sentence Poems*, *Oxford Magazine*, *White Knuckle Press* and *Yellow Chair Review* to name a few.

Nixes Mate Books features small-batch artisanal literature, created by writers that use all 26 letters of the alphabet and then some, honing their craft the time-honored way: one line at a time.

More Nixes Mate titles:
ON BROAD SOUND | Rusty Barnes
KINKY KEEPS THE HOUSE CLEAN | Mari Deweese
SQUALL LINE ON THE HORIZON | Pris Campbell
COMES TO THIS | Jeff Weddle
HITCHHIKING BEATITUDES | Michael McInnis
AIR & OTHER STORIES | Lauren Leja
WAITING FOR AN ANSWER | Heather Sullivan
A WORLD WHERE | Paul Brookes
MY SOUTHERN CHILDHOOD | Pris Campbell
THE PAUL BUNYAN BALLROOM | Bud Backen
NIXES MATE REVIEW ANTHOLOGY 2016/17
CAPP ROAD | Matt Borczon
THE WILLOW HOWL | Lisa Brognano
JESUS IN THE GHOST ROOM | Rusty Barnes
HEART OF THE BROKEN WORLD | Jeff Weddle
STARLAND | Jessica Purdy

Forthcoming titles from Nixes Mate:
LUBBOCK ELECTRIC | Anne Elezabeth Pluto
LABOR | Lisa DeSiro
HE WAS A GOOD FATHER | Mark Borczon

nixesmate.pub/books

www.ingramcontent.com/pod-product-compliance
Lightning Source LLC
Chambersburg PA
CBHW050546300426
44113CB00012B/2289